BALANCING LIFE IN STILETTOS

Learning to Live Beyond Abuse

Dawna Elguera

Copyright © 2018 by Dawna Elguera

Balancing Life In Stilettos:
Learning to Live Beyond Abuse

All rights reserved. This book or any portion thereof may not be reproduced or used in any manner whatsoever without the express written permission of the publisher except for the use of brief quotations in a book review.

Scripture quotations used in this book are from the following sources and used with permission: Unless otherwise indicated, all Scripture is taken from the New King James Version®.

Copyright © 1982 by Thomas Nelson. Used by permission. All rights reserved.

Ordering Information:
Books are available on Amazon.com
Printed in the United States of America
First Printing, January 2018
ISBN-13: 978-0984562039
ISBN-10: 0984562036

The Rock Church
75400 Gerald Ford Dr. Ste. 110
Palm Desert, CA, 92211
www.DawnaElguera.com

BALANCING LIFE IN STILETTOS

Contents

Dedication vii

Introduction ix

Chapter 1: It's A Girl! 1

Chapter 2: Sticks And Stones 7

Chapter 3: The Roof Is On Fire 23

Chapter 4: My Prince Charming 31

Chapter 5: Life As A Neat Freak 39

Chapter 6: Mirror, Mirror 47

Chapter 7: Ashes, Ashes, We All Fall Down 59

Chapter 8: The Higher The Heel, The Closer To God 69

Chapter 9: Defying The Law Of Gravity 75

Chapter 10: They Lived Happily Ever After 81

Notes 87

About The Author 89

Dedication

With a heart full of gratitude, I thank my husband Eddie for never giving up on me and for loving me through the good, bad, and the ugly! To my sons Malachi, Christopher, and Isaac, and their wives Melissa and Lana, Thank You for encouraging me to tell my story in book form, even when I didn't think anyone would want to read it. I am so grateful to my family for believing that by me being transparent enough to tell my story, someone else's life could benefit. I love you all from the depths of my heart!! I also thank my friends and church family at The Rock Church. I appreciate you allowing me to tell my story with no judgment or criticism, but rather you cheered me on while praying that anyone who reads my story might be impacted for the better. To my extended family who played a part in rescuing me from what could've been an unimaginable life for a child, Thank you! And to the many friends who kept telling me over the years that I must write a book and tell my story…here you go! Thank you for pushing me!!

I did it!!

Introduction

I've always wanted to be taller. Even as a little girl, back in the early '70's I would walk around in my grandmother's platform shoes. As a teen, I always wore heels. I actually stopped growing in junior high school. Not fair, right!? Being petite with blonde hair and blue eyes, you couldn't even consider me a life-sized Barbie doll– you would instead consider me to be more like a "Child-sized" Barbie, since. I only grew to the whopping height of 5 feet 2 inches tall. I was always too short for "Something." Perhaps I thought that if I was taller, no one could abuse me. Or perhaps I just wanted to be "tall enough" for whatever adventure I faced at the time.

I remember my grandmother always telling me that I wasn't tall enough for the dream jobs that I wanted in the future. I wasn't tall enough to be a flight attendant. I wasn't tall enough to be a model. I wasn't even tall enough to reach the top shelves in the kitchen.

As I grew older, my shoe of choice was always something with a heel. The only time I could be seen in athletic shoes was for gym class. By high school, every outfit had a coordinating pair of stilettos and a matching purse. I believe that the right pair of shoes can pull any outfit together. If you don't think that a great pair of heels can make a difference, go back and read the stories of Cinderella and Dorothy!

So why did I title this book Balancing Life in Stilettos? We all go through life with many things that we must balance. Everywhere around us we are being told to live a balanced life. As modern women, we are often expected to "balance a career and a family". Even with all the stress, We are told that we need to discover a "healthy balance." Even Dr. Seuss tells us that "Life's a Great Balancing Act."

For me, I feel like my life has been a series of good and bad experiences that I have learned how to not just face, to overcome and balance the past with the present so that I can have a greater future. All this while wearing a great pair of stilettos!

So just like how we learn to walk upright and stable in a beautiful pair of heels, I believe that we can learn to walk with our shoulders back and our heads held high in confidence, as we step into a future that is not determined by our past. but a beautiful future that we chose to live despite our past!

So, slip on your fabulous stilettos and let's live a fabulous life, ladies!

"So be sure when you step,

step with care and great tact.

And remember that life's a Great Balancing Act.

And will you succeed?

Yes! You will, indeed!

(98 and ¾ percent guaranteed)

Kid, you'll move mountains."

— Dr Seuss, excerpted from
Oh, the Places You'll Go

Chapter 1

IT'S A GIRL!

"Is everyone ready for this?" the nurse asked the young expecting parents and both sets of grandparents who had rallied together with excitement in the examination room. My oldest son and his wife were expecting their first child, and my daughter-in-law was about 20 weeks pregnant. They had scheduled a special day for us all to meet at her ultrasound appointment to find out if they were having a girl or a boy. This would be the first grandchild for my husband and me, as well as the first child for my son and his wife. I wanted to do something special for this day, so I had two gifts waiting for this momentous occasion, a little blue outfit and a little pink outfit.

The ultrasound tech moved the wand around Melissa's belly. "The heart looks healthy." she said. "Here's the profile. Look, the baby is waving at you!" I felt as if the tech was teasing us, making us wait with anticipation. But then, the moment when we would find out finally arrived. The moment that would determine which gift I would be giving these young, first time, expectant parents and which would be getting returned. With one swift maneuvering of the medical instrument, the tech said, "There you go! Can anyone tell what it is?"

We all cheered as the announcement was made. "It's a girl!"

Tears and cheers exploded as we all celebrated that a precious little pink bundle of joy would forever change our lives. This was such an exciting experience to be part of since the experience my own parents had was much different.

Forty-five years earlier, two young lovers announced to their family that they were expecting their first child, but the knowledge of my impending arrival was far from a glorious celebration. You would think that it would be an exciting time for their families. I would be the first grandchild on both sides of the family. But the circumstances in the mid-1960s were very different.

My parents weren't married when I was conceived. They were only 19 when they met. In fact, my mom was actually on a date with my dad's friend, but my dad caught her eye. He was quite a charmer! He looked like James Dean, a young actor and heartthrob in the 1950s. My mom was a vivacious woman who made friends easily. She was a beautiful petite blonde with blue eyes who always seemed to be the life of any party. At the time they started dating they lived in California and were now barely in their twenties. And much to the chagrin of their parents, they hadn't known each other very long. Before I was born, they ran off to live in "Sin City" Las Vegas. To support their new life in Las Vegas, my dad became a blackjack dealer in one of the Vegas casinos.

My mother was considered physically challenged because she wore a brace on her left leg, due to polio she contracted as a child. She had been hit by a car while playing in the street when she was just four years old, and before her little body had a chance to fully recover, she contracted polio. Back in the early 1950s, the polio virus was at an all-time high. It caused paralysis in a person's body. My mother was fortunate that the virus only attacked her left leg, which had been weakened by the car accident. But due to the limited understanding of the illness at that time, doctors assumed that it would affect her ability to conceive children. Because of this, getting pregnant and becoming a mother wasn't something that my mom ever expected to experience for herself. Fortunately, the doctors were wrong. And as one would expect, she, along with my dad, were both overjoyed at the discovery that she was pregnant.

The family, on the other hand, was apprehensive. Some relatives thought she should terminate the pregnancy. Others tried to convince her that if she and the baby survived, she should give the baby away, citing that she would be unable to care for the child properly. In those days it was not so easy for a handicapped person to get a job.

Against all the odds, on October 29, 1966, the same announcement was made by a doctor in a Las Vegas delivery room: "It's a girl!" Elated first-time parents celebrated the announcement. I would be the only child that my mother would ever have—her pride and joy. Her little pink bundle of love. Little did my mother know the challenges that her precious little girl would face in the future.

Five generations on my mom's side

Chapter 2

STICKS AND STONES

As children, many of us sang this silly little song as a way of letting others know that we wouldn't cower to the futile attempt at bullying and abuse at the mercy of name callers. "Sticks and stones may break my bones, but names will never hurt me." Unfortunately, there is no such song for many other forms of abuse. And I learned this much too early in life.

Let me just say, as I begin to write this chapter; I waited to write the story of my abuse until both of my parents had passed away. They would've been hurt and angry to learn that people they loved and trusted could betray their trust in such a way. It would have been too devastating for them to hear all that I kept a secret over the years. And, to be completely honest, I was a bit afraid that my mom would've wanted to kill the men who violated me.

Sticks and stones

may break my bones,

but names will never

hurt me.

My parents finally got married in a civil ceremony when I was about three years old. They moved back to California to help my dad's parents manage their hotel and property management businesses. By this time my dad had started drinking heavily and my mom's need for prescription medication, stemming from the residual effects of polio, had escalated. My parents ended up separating when I was four years old. The way my mom told the story, the cause of the divorce was because she wouldn't give my dad money for alcohol because she needed it to buy food for me. The divorce and custody battle ended up dragging on for a couple of years after this incident. In the interim, I was moved around from family member to family member because neither of my parents was really in a good condition to care for me, because of their individual addictions.

Statistics show that most children who are abused never tell anyone. I can say from first-hand experience that this is a fact. However, there are still living family members who will be shocked, some ashamed, and some relieved to read my story. Those who will be relieved are the ones who suspected that things were not right and worked together with others to rescue from pretty unhealthy situations, although I believe they never knew about the sexual abuse at the hands of family members. Those who will be ashamed are family members who should've known better, but chose to make the wrong decisions. They will remain unnamed in this book, but their actions of sexual and physical abuse cannot be erased or forgotten. Those who will be shocked never had a clue, and I don't blame them for that.

Before I go any further, let's just establish the official legal definition of abuse[1].

Everything that is contrary to good order established by usage, departure from reasonable use, immoderate or improper use, physical or mental maltreatment, Misuse, and deception, to wrong in speech, reproach coarsely, disparage, revile, and malign.

Now for the legal definition of child abuse[2].

Physical, sexual, or emotional mistreatment or neglect of a child, an act, or failure to act, on the part of a parent or caretaker that results in the death, serious physical or emotional harm, Sexual Abuse, or exploitation of a child, or which places the child in an imminent risk of serious harm.

Websters Dictionary uses the following terms to define abuse[3].

(Verb) – To treat in a harsh or harmful way, to use or treat in a way that causes damage, to use wrongly, a corrupt practice or custom, improper or excessive use or treatment, misuse, to use so as to injure or damage, to attack in words, revile, to use insulting, coarse, or bad language about or to (Noun) – language that condemns or vilifies usually unjustly, intemperately, and angrily, improper treatment, physical maltreatment, wrong, bad or excessive use, injury, insulting or coarse language, a bad, unjust or corrupt custom or practice

Many people experience some form of abuse during their life. Some of the most common types of abuse are: sexual, verbal, physical, and emotional. I don't like to say that people are victims because I believe that being a victim is a mindset and a choice. We each have a choice as to how we respond to circumstances in our lives. Regardless of how abuse takes form in someone's life, it is not right and causes many other issues to manifest. Many end up dealing with control issues and/or rejection issues. Others try to numb the pain through alcohol, drugs, or other self-destructive behavior. Some end up repeating the same abusive behavior on others. I am so happy that I never struggled with addiction. I dabbled socially, but drugs and alcohol were never really appealing to me because I saw the effects it had on my parents. It has been important to me that I break that cycle in our family and for future generations.

The first time I realized there were wounds that couldn't be fixed by a nursery rhyme or a cute little song, I hadn't even entered Kindergarten yet. Each time I think back to those events in my early childhood, they play back in my head like a nightmare, like I am on the outside of the situation watching it like a bad movie. But all the feelings of fear and powerlessness flood back as if it were happening all over again.

There was never a "grooming period" in my situation. My abusers were family and men who were trusted and everyone assumed it was "safe" for me to be around them. It was always about the timing. They would catch me in a location. Trapped and isolated. The first time it ever happened, I was locked in a dark bathroom by a family member and forced to do things that no child should ever be part of. He turned off the lights and said that he wouldn't turn on the lights and unlock the door until I did what he wanted. I can't remember if there were other family members home, it may have been a family gathering. And it was a two-story house, so others would have been preoccupied. But I do remember the last words I was told before he unlocked the door and was let out of that dark bathroom: "Don't ever tell anyone." He soon moved away, and so did I.

Years later, as a young teenager, I brought this up to the perpetrator and said, "I still remember what you made me do."

His response was once again, "Don't ever tell anyone." The saddest part is that those four words have such powerful psychological implications that have silenced many people over the years, both young and old.

I'm not proud of the fact that I never told anyone when I was younger. I waited until after my parents passed away before talking about it publicly. After I got married I told my husband what had happened. He was very sweet about it, but I don't think he knew what to do with the information. He just took my lead as to how to respond to the information he had just been given. It was important for him to understand why I was so protective of our children. Also, for the health of our marriage, I believe that he needed to have an understanding of the sexual abuse I experienced as a child, as well as the physical abuse that I went through as a teenager. As a teenager, I also told some of my friends about the physical abuse that I was dealing with. My dad confessed to me, years later, that a couple of them had told their parents and that my dad had been questioned about it. He apologized for not doing anything at the time. I believe that speaking up and telling someone what has happened to you is crucial. However, I understand why many never say anything. It is a very scary thing to speak up and tell someone. But sometimes by speaking up, you can save yourself or even help save someone else from further abuse by the person who abused you.

Time runs together as a blur for me. It's difficult to remember specific ages. But, there would be other occurrences of sexual abuse during my childhood while still in elementary school, with a different family member. I remember getting out of bed and curling up into a ball in a pile of dirty laundry so I couldn't be found by him so that he wouldn't touch me anymore. As I got older, I learned to create boundaries and keep a distance from those who had sexually abused me when I was younger. Unfortunately, the boundaries didn't help with nightmares. The abuse had caused me to suffer from paralyzing night terrors, which started in elementary school and continued into my early teen years. It also caused a fear of enclosed spaces, (claustrophobia) and anxiety.

I didn't realize that the severity of the situations my mom had placed me in as a child hadn't gone unnoticed until the day I found letters written between one of my aunts and my grandmother on my dad's side. Pieces began to fall into place once I read Comments that had been made regarding my safety. There were little jokes about trying to convince my mom that I wasn't hers. And I recalled memories of living with various family members, and living in places where friends of my grandmother "just happened to live nearby."

I used to think it was strange that friends of mine would talk about memories of their childhood, but I had very little memories, only little mental snapshots. My snapshots were mostly happy memories. But as I look back as an adult and parent, I realize that behind the memories were scenarios that, as an adult, I would not feel comfortable having my children in.

I remember living in an apartment with my mom and her "husband." I remember getting my tonsils out and getting to eat popsicles and Jell-O. Every child's dream! I remember that while I was at home recovering, our dog was having puppies in my closet. But then, as I think back to the bigger picture, the apartment that we lived in was in an apartment complex that was owned and occupied by a motorcycle gang. The gang that my mom's husband was part of. I have memories of riding on the back of Harley's. I even have a scar to remind me of that time in my childhood—a physical scar on my right ankle from an exhaust pipe burn. And I remember conversations about members of the group being in jail for robbing or killing people. Not quite the average childhood memory!

I also remember a time when my mom and her last husband lived on a military base. One summer, in particular, I remember my mom sharing with me that if anyone ever came to the door, that before I opened the door, I should cover a certain "home garden" that she had in the kitchen because she was growing "magic" mushrooms. And I don't mean the cooking kind. These were the type of mushrooms that people eat to hallucinate.

When I was in early elementary we had a special time where my mother taught me some important life lessons. One of which was how to roll the perfect joint. Not too thick, not too thin, and not pregnant in the middle.

Then there was the hitchhiking, the line of men coming in and out of her house. Her need to jump out of the car at an intersection to get into a fight with men who were driving recklessly. And all the times that I spent hanging out at bars with her although I did learn to shoot a pretty good game of pool.

Me at the Honolulu Zoo age 7ish

At the time I didn't understand the true purpose of my new pair of roller-skates when I started first grade. But I just remember my dad telling me that as

I roller-skated home from school I needed to watch out for my mom and her friends trying to give me a ride home. He told me that if I saw my mom that I should skate home as fast as I could and not get into the car. It must have all tied into one of the letters that I found in an old box. My aunt and my grandmother were trying to figure out how to get me out of my mom's care because the living conditions were not healthy for a child.

My dad was eventually granted custody of me and we moved to the mountains of Lake Arrowhead, California. My dad thought that it would be the safest place to raise a little girl, as a single father. Although my dad was still struggling with alcohol addiction, life seemed to be settling down. He remarried when I was in the sixth grade.

I am thankful that when I was a young teenager, my dad began taking our family to church. It was there that I discovered comforting scriptures that I have been able to speak over myself to help when anxiety is triggered. That being said, healing is an ongoing process.

To this day, there are some types of enclosed spaces that I cannot enter. Elevators, walk-in coolers, anything that I feel I wouldn't be able to get myself out of. I even had a panic attack one time when trying to go through a cornfield maze with our boys. My family jokes about how I always look for the escape hatch in elevators. It all stems back to not having the control to get out of that dark bathroom as a little girl. Thankfully I have been able to identify and work through how past situations caused certain types of fear and anxiety that have manifested in my life over the years.

Fortunately, life situations created distance from my sexual abusers, either through a job change, which moved them, or my relocation once my dad won custody of me. Either way, I had been rescued! Or so I thought.

As I grew older, the type of abuse changed, along with who the abusers were. My dad eventually remarried. What had initially seemed like a wonderful thing, soon took a dark turn. The abuse became physical and verbal instead of sexual. And it was no longer just male family members, but my stepmother. But, just as when I was younger, I once again realized that even though I could sing the song, it still didn't stop the hurting.

The healing is ongoing. The church became a place where I was able to learn coping skills and the ability to find my own voice and strength. It taught me how to be more self-aware. I learned that as I identify triggers, I could pray for wisdom and speak faith and healing in newly recognized strongholds. This is as a result of the Holy Spirit that dwells within me. I refuse to allow the devil to win in any area of my life because I've already attained victory through my salvation

I fully believe that people who have gone through or are still going through abuse don't have to suffer in silence. I believe that freedom and healing are available. Only God can bring complete healing and restoration to the inner wounds, the trauma, and the past pain through the power of the Holy Spirit. It will take time and commitment to work through the residual effects of the abuse.

You or someone you know might secretly be dealing with abuse. I want you to know that what happened in the past, or what may be happening right now, doesn't have to be part of your future. Freedom and healing are possible.

Chapter 3

THE ROOF IS ON FIRE

I can still remember the first time that my stepmother hit me. I wasn't even in my teens yet. I was only ten years old and it was the day of my grandmother's funeral (my dad's mother). I was sitting in the living room and was so sad that I was not allowed to attend. My stepmother said that it wasn't a place for children. My dad was still drinking at this time, so I don't think he was even in a condition to make decisions, so my stepmother, who had two children of her own, took control of the family.

On that day, as I sat on the couch mourning, I guess she mistook my sadness for disrespect, because she stormed up to me and slapped me across the face, and told me never to disrespect her again. Needless to say, I was shocked, stunned, and confused. She sent me to my room to think about what I had done and change my behavior. So I spent that time with my head reeling and trying to figure out what I had done. Little did I know at that point that it was just the beginning of the abuse that was to come.

When my dad married my stepmother, she already had a son and daughter of her own who were both younger than me, so I was no longer an only child. Then she became pregnant and gave birth to a boy. So now my dad had a son. This created even more of a disconnect between my dad and me. There was an eleven-year gap between my half-brother and me. One would think that a baby would bring joy and peace to the family, but on the contrary, anger, strife, and violence continued in the home. I didn't realize at the time, but my stepmother was also violent with my dad as well. I never saw her hit either of her own children.

One night she was driving around town with a shotgun in her car, trying to track my dad down as he was bar hopping because she was going to kill him. I have no idea what caused her to get that angry. And I don't know why she changed her mind and didn't follow through with her plan. But my dad lived to tell the story. Coincidentally, this was the night that my dad decided to stop drinking and determined that we needed to go to church as a family.

At the age of sixteen everything had come to a breaking point. One day, I was in my bedroom when my stepmother came bursting through the doorway (this had become a common occurrence. It was usually when I was in either my bathroom or bedroom). I don't even know what the problem was, but she was upset about something. Anyway, she proceeded to start swinging, grabbing, shaking, yelling, and scratching. The accompanying verbal barrage of degrading statements was usually the same list of comparisons, telling me that, because she was a certain way when she was younger, that she was convinced I must be the same way. Now as I look back, I think she may have been bi-polar. But back then, I don't think there was a diagnosis for that.

Over the years I had begun trying to protect myself, which was a bit of a lost cause because she was taller than me, and about three times my size in weight. (Keep in mind that I was only 5'2" and weighed less than 100 pounds.) I'm not sure what her childhood was like, or why she would compare me to her. I don't know if her anger was based on jealousy, insecurity, or just plain meanness, but either way, she had some deranged idea that I was some promiscuous, untrustworthy girl that was going to end up on drugs or prostituting myself on a street corner somewhere. Again, I think these episodes of rage may have been caused by a bipolar disorder on her part.

At some point, my dad arrived, and as usual just stood in the doorway, watching in silence, expressionless. I'm not quite sure why he was watching because he would never intervene. I guess it would've just caused more strife between them.

To this day, I cannot ever remember what always set off my stepmother. But after this particular incident, after she stormed out of the room, and I was left standing there with bruises developing and my arms bloody from her grabbing and shaking me and digging her fingernails deep into my skin, my dad lingered behind and made (what he thought was) an apology. The words that came out of his mouth pierced me to the very core. It was with the following words that I knew I had to get out of the house, or things would continue to get worse. He said, "I'm sorry, but I can't defend you. She is my wife, and I've made a covenant with God. She will be my wife forever, but you're just my daughter, and you'll be out of the house soon." I don't think he realized how prophetic those words would become.

I knew I had to make a change, so I immediately ran to a neighbor's house and called my mom. I told her a mild version of what happened and asked if I could move to Colorado and live with her. She agreed, so we made plans for me to move to Colorado as soon as possible. I went back to my dad's house and told him that I was moving to Colorado with my mom. My stepmother's response was a classic threat: "If you walk out of this door, you can never come back in." Needless to say, I was happy to oblige. I packed up my things and stayed with a friend until I was able to make travel arrangements. It would be years later before my dad admitted that some of his friends knew about the abuse and told him they were aware of it. But no one ever did anything about it.

Sometimes your pain

Screams louder

Than

Your purpose.

I didn't learn until I was an adult and married, that after each incident, my step-mother would run to one of her "church friend's" homes to cry and complain about what a horrible teenager I was. It makes sense now, in hindsight, why many of her friends were a bit standoffish with me.

One thing that I was grateful for, in all this, was that we were still going to church every time the doors were open. I realized early on that going to church isn't going to cause God to sprinkle magic fairy dust on me and remove all my problems. Instead, I realized that it was all based on what I was willing to learn and actually apply to my life. Because it was there, sitting in church, that I would learn such powerful tools that helped me to separate what was being done and said to me, from the truth of God's plan and purpose for my life. I realize that some people have a hard time reconciling how a loving God could allow such things to happen. Many people get mad at God and turn away from Him and the church because they feel that God or someone in the church should have intervened or protected them from what happened to them. I don't know exactly how or why I was able to separate God and church from the abuse that took place. But I believe that everyone is responsible for his or her own actions.

As I read about people in the Bible who were in desperate situations, God didn't rescue them OUT OF the situations, but he gave them peace in the midst of the situations. So I adopted that philosophy into my own life. I searched for how I could find peace within myself. I searched for how I could find peace in the midst of the storm in my life. I began to read through my Bible and discovered scriptures that would describe a God who loved me. A God who created me with a beautiful life in mind. A God who didn't want any harm to come to me, but on the contrary, wanted me to live a life of joy and peace. A

God who said, in Jeremiah 29:11; "For I know the thoughts that I think toward you, thoughts of peace and not of evil, to give you a future and a hope." As I read about this incredible God, I wanted to learn more! I began to realize that my past didn't determine my future. I started to learn that I was created in His image and that I was created with an incredible plan, purpose, and destiny for my life.

So, that summer, at the age of 16, I walked out of my dad's house and made the move from Lake Arrowhead, California, to Colorado Springs, Colorado. I enrolled for my senior year at Cheyenne Mountain High School, with the goal of a new life.

"For I know the thoughts that
I think toward you, says
the Lord, thoughts of peace
and not of evil, to give you a
future and a hope."
Jeremiah 29:11

Chapter 4

MY PRINCE CHARMING

I celebrated my seventeenth birthday with my new friends in Colorado Springs, Colorado. I'd been attending Cheyenne Mountain High School, with a goal to live a new and different life. I've always been an outgoing person, in spite of the abuse. So starting a new school was an exciting adventure! I made friends quickly, which helped me to hear of all the great opportunities for me around the school. So I ran for Student Council and won. I joined the Senior Girls Club, enrolled in a public speaking class, took a computer programming class, made tons of new friends, and thoroughly engrossed myself in my new life away from the abuse.

It was different living with my mom. She loved me and was very encouraging. However, she enjoyed the party life. Drinking and drugs were the norm at her house. The interesting thing is that my grandmother and grandfather lived across the street. So I was able to spend time at their house for a calmer atmosphere. All through the months that I spent in Colorado with my mom, the conversation of what happened with my stepmother never came up. I guess all that mattered was that I was away from my stepmother.

By the time Christmas rolled around, I had begun to miss home. Not my dad's house, but my home church, and my friends in California. I missed sitting in the services and hearing about the amazing God who created me. I missed sitting in an atmosphere where other people were discovering the same life-changing concepts that I had learned. I don't know why I never sought out a new church in Colorado Springs. I just missed the church where I had learned so much about God and myself. So I called my dad and explained that I was thinking about moving back to California. Because my stepmother had made it clear that I wasn't welcome to live in their house anymore, he suggested that I talk to a beautiful couple, Mike and Carol, that were part of our church who ran a ministry home. This home was owned by a Christian couple who offered rooms in their home for people who were new Christians, or who had gone through a tough time and needed housing. They had house rules that included church attendance, group Bible study, discipleship, and curfews. I called, they said that they had a room, and I was welcome to move in. So over Christmas break, I packed up everything at my mom's house and headed back to California.

Could I have joined a church in Colorado Springs? Probably! I had also been attending a Christian Bible Study group at then, named Colorado College. But, I needed more! I needed what was familiar. I tried to explain it to my grandmother, but she didn't understand. I tried to explain it to my mom, but she didn't understand. I'm not sure I even fully understood why it was so important for me to go back to the little mountain community of Lake Arrowhead, California.

I moved back home, enrolled back into school, found a job, and began working to pay for my room and board at the ministry home. My dad helped me to buy a car so that I could get to and from work and school. I settled into a very routine life of work, school, and church. I worked extra hard to finish up school a couple of months early and graduated in April so that I could work full time. Although things were never the same between, dad, my stepmother, and me we had a cordial relationship with each other.

One day when I came home from work, Carol told me that she had been talking to a woman at work. The woman she was talking to also attended our church. Carol proceeded to tell this woman about me. And as they spoke, the woman began to tell Carol about her son. I immediately knew where this conversation was headed. I told Carol, "I am not interested in dating anyone at this time. It's just Jesus and me right now! I want to take time for me. To grow stronger in my relationship with God. I don't want to meet any guy. I don't want to date. It's not going to happen." I had dated a little bit during high school, but it just wasn't a focus for me at the time. I had been going through a lot of upheaval and change in my life over the past year, and just wanted to get centered and focused on a healthy and peaceful life.

Carol said, "That's fine, you don't have to meet anyone or date anyone. But why don't you go with me to a Bible Study on Thursday night at their restaurant?" I agreed to attend the Bible Study. After all, what harm could come from attending a Bible Study?

It was at that Bible study that I met a guy named Eddie Elguera. He was a few years older than me and attractive, which was nice, but I wasn't seeking a boyfriend. He was tall and neatly dressed. He had dark hair, dark kind eyes, and a gentle smile. He was very shy, but he was excited about the things of God, which was refreshing!

There were only about ten people in attendance. The Bible Study was led by a lovely older woman who had an infectious passion for helping others live a successful life in God. Her name was May Hubolt and she was an evangelist at heart. She lived in Huntington Beach and would spend her days telling people about Jesus. Then she would drive up to our little town of Lake Arrowhead and do Bible Studies with the Elguera family and a few others who were eager to learn more about God.

After the Bible Study was over, Eddie asked me if I would be interested in going to dinner the next evening. I figured a girl has to eat! So I agreed to dinner. After dinner, he dropped me back off at home. I was so impressed that he was such a gentleman! It was so unlike my usual experiences with guys. It seems like guys always wanted a sexual relationship and I didn't. It's no wonder that I didn't want to date. But Eddie was different. He didn't try to sneak a kiss, and he didn't try to put his arm around me, he didn't even try to hold my hand. He was a complete gentleman.

As time went on, I agreed to more dates. He was shy but easy to talk to. It was refreshing to be with someone who seemed to be as excited about living a life for God as I was.

We officially started dating, and after a few months, we realized that this was headed toward marriage. I had indeed met my prince charming! Little did I know that real life is not a fairytale like what we see in the movies.

Balancing Life in Stilettos

Eddie and I in Seattle early 1990's

Chapter 5

LIFE AS A NEAT FREAK

Order and cleanliness is a beautiful thing. Some even throw around the phrase "Cleanliness is next to Godliness." But for me, cleanliness, order, and organization were more than just a matter of character or good personal hygiene. Clinically it could be labeled as Obsessive Compulsive Disorder or O.C.D. For me, this was birthed out of a need to control my surroundings, and have some structure that I was in control.

Of course, at the time, I had no concept of Obsessive Compulsive Disorder or the connection between abuse and O.C.D. until I was an adult. Researchers have found that there is a link between O.C.D. and childhood trauma. There are times, even now, when I am under an immense amount of stress, that I realize that the need for order becomes overwhelming.

It never really seemed like it was a problem. I mean, come on! Don't all parents want their kids to keep their rooms clean? However, I took it to the next level. My closet was all color coordinated, from light to dark. All the shirts together (short sleeves together, and long sleeves together, of course.) All pants together. You get the idea. My drawers were all organized. My bed was made every morning right after I got up. I never had to be asked or told to clean my room. Unfortunately, my room was so organized that it made it easier for others to go through my things when I wasn't around. Whether it was my stepmother snooping for who-knows-what, or my step-sister taking my clothes, or my step-brother stealing money and other things.

The downside of O.C.D. is that if things weren't perfect, or if situations become too overwhelming, I would tend to retreat. I would avoid what seems overwhelming to me. I still have a tendency to do this. It is important that I recognize when things (clutter, disorganization, etc.) are beginning to reach a level of being too overwhelming for me. When I'm able to recognize myself getting overwhelmed with disorganization, I need to set aside time to work on it, or I call a friend to come and help me get over the hump by assisting me in getting things back into a manageable place. I need order and organization!

I realized that having parents that both had their own dysfunctions, including hoarding (they would call it collecting), caused me to need to be organized throughout my childhood, teen years, and even into adulthood. Moving was easy because I could keep all of my belongings in just a couple of boxes and a suitcase. Getting married was another adjustment in learning how to not only keep my stuff organized but now account for belongings of another person. I don't think it ever affected my social life though. I was just always a very "put together" person.

Having children brought on a whole new level of O.C.D! When I think back to when my boys were small, I can still smell the Pine Sol. I can hear the boys playing in the background, as I am on my hands and knees in the kitchen with a bucket of Pine Sol and water solution next to me. With a clean towel in hand, I begin at one corner of the kitchen floor and start to work my way across the kitchen. I still remember the thought that would drift through my head, "As long as I can keep the floor clean, I won't have to worry about the boys dropping food on the floor and then picking it up and putting it in their mouths because I've washed away all the germs." As I finished the kitchen floor, I would make my way to the entryway near the front door, and then to the other non-carpeted floors throughout the house. And then, I would bring out the vacuum. I don't know about you, but I love to see the lines that are left on a freshly vacuumed carpet! This was my daily routine, and it brought me a sense of joy. And my husband always enjoyed coming home to a clean house.

Structure and order

are

beautiful things!

I didn't really think anything bad about it all until I began to see some of the same tendencies start to manifest in my children. My oldest son would have meltdowns if his clothes weren't the exact same color, or if his hands got dirty. As my second oldest entered school, I began to see him struggle with mistakes he made while doing his homework. He would get angry, crumple up his work, and start all over again. I realized that I needed to model a less perfectionist example for my boys. At times I had to talk them through being frustrated because things weren't perfect, even to the color of their clothes needing to match. It seems funny now, but I had to teach them that it was okay to have different color stripes on their shirt or socks as long as there was at least one color that matched their pants. For me, it was a process of allowing little mistakes or messes. I had to talk myself through situations and like my husband would say, "Just close the door and don't look at the mess." Not that I became a slob. But realizing that it was okay if there were "organized piles" on his desk, or if the clothes in the closet weren't all on matching hangers.

I realize that this chapter may seem like a silly thing to talk about, but in all reality, we must recognize when these types of situations become a controlling factor in our lives. It's great to be clean and organized. Structure and order are beautiful things! However, when they begin to control you, instead of you controlling it, then it becomes a problem that needs to be addressed. It was important for me to look at the bigger picture and realize why I needed order and structure in my life. I realized that it all came back to needing something that I could be in control of. This all boiled down to because of my abuse as a child and teenager, circumstances which I had no control over. It caused a need to be in control of something. For me, it was my surroundings. For you or someone else, there may be other things that you deal with as a result of abuse. However, the good news is that if we can identify these behaviors, we can learn skills to better deal with them.

Balancing Life in Stilettos

Our growing little family in 1988

Chapter 6

MIRROR, MIRROR

Over the years, my husband and I became youth pastors at our church. In the early years of being youth pastors, I took a Lay Counseling course on Crisis Counseling. Because of my past, the subject fascinated me. And where we lived was surrounded by cities with some tough neighborhoods, so I thought it might come in handy. Aside from the certificate I received from the Crisis Counseling course, I eventually went on to earn a Bachelor's Degree in Biblical Studies. I didn't realize at the time that it would all come in handy in the future. It wasn't long before I had women and young girls requesting to meet with me at the church who had been through sexual or physical abuse in their lives. So along with my various responsibilities at the church, I found myself helping others to walk through similar situations as mine. I believe that if we are able to overcome difficult situations in our lives, we will have opportunities to help others. I never have, nor do I now, call myself a counselor. What I do is give "Spiritual Guidance." I share from a Biblical perspective, as well as my own experiences. And I am always careful to encourage people to seek professional counseling. Even though I wasn't able to benefit from access to professional counseling until I was an adult, I still acknowledge the need and benefits for others.

By 2006 the church that we were part of had grown from a small 12 person Bible study to a 19,000 member church. Our youth ministry had grown to 1,000 teens attending weekly. During the year of 2006, my husband and I were asked to launch a new church in the Palm Springs area of Southern California. It was an exciting new adventure for our family. As we stepped into the role of Senior Pastors, little did I know that this would also be the place where God would begin my journey of writing this book!

A few years after we began pastoring the new church, a mom brought her daughter in to speak with me. The young girl sat across from me in my little office at the church. Her mother sat next to her and started to share with me the reason they asked to visit with me. As the mother spoke, the 16-year-old girl sat quietly, her body shaking, tears rolling down her face, her shoulders hunched over, and eyes focused on the floor in front of her. The mother shared that her daughter had recently faced a devastating situation at work.

I asked the young girl to share with me what happened. She told me she had been raped by her boss just a few months earlier and now had to face him in court. "I don't know how I can face him again," she said. "I don't know how I can move on from this. I know the Bible says I have to forgive him, but I don't know how." Yes, she said the "F" word…forgiveness! Hmm… forgiveness. The memories of being so violated came flooding back. The fear, the pain, the feeling of violation. I can't help but get a little angry that another girl must face something so devastating. I began to think about how tough that word is. Forgiveness. It's a word that seems so easy to talk about, but very challenging to do. How does someone move on from something like this? How does someone begin the process of forgiveness?

So, as this sweet girl sat across from me, I began to tell my story. I told her of how my abusers were family members. I spoke about feeling trapped because at the time I didn't know how to create boundaries and felt forced to see my abusers during family gatherings. I told her that I completely understood the feeling of hopelessness and anxiety. I understood waking up from tormenting nightmares that I could not escape from.

And with a look of desperation on her face, the young girl asked, "How did you forgive?"

My response was, "Oh sweetie! Don't feel pressured to forgive right away. It takes time. And it's not the same timeline for everyone. It may seem like it was easy for me, but it's only because I've had over forty years of practice, and you've just begun your journey of forgiveness." I'm not sure if she was being told that she had to forgive right away, or if it was something that she felt personally that she needed to do. But I don't believe that anyone should ever push a specific timeline of forgiveness on someone else. "There is no due date on forgiveness."

I went on to share that the choice to forgive is exactly that, a choice. Is it easy? No! But it's necessary, necessary for your healing and well being. At some point in your process, it may become a necessary choice that you must consciously make minute to minute. Then eventually it will become an hour-to-hour thing, then day to day, etc. Forgiveness is not a destination, but a journey of decisions that you must choose to make each time the negative thoughts begin to enter your mind. Each time the re-runs of events try to play again and again in your mind, you must stop the thoughts and take charge of your thought process immediately!

Throughout my childhood, between the ages of nine to thirteen, I would awaken from paralyzing nightmares that would torment me night after night. It was always the same nightmare. I was in a large dark room with large windows all around. And I could sense someone was looking in at me, but I could not tell which direction they were coming from. I would try to hide, but there was nowhere to hide. In my nightmare I would try to lie down, as close to the wall under the windows as possible, to try not to be seen, but the overwhelming sense of fear and powerlessness would overtake me. I would eventually wake up, unable to move, or scream, or do anything but lay there feeling my heart beating so hard that it felt as if it was going to jump out of my chest. It beat so hard it seemed as though I could hear it beating in my ears.

This went on for years until something happened. Something that would, drastically, forever change my life! I began to read the Bible and learn helpful concepts of prayer. It all started when my dad had a dramatic life-changing encounter with God. The way my dad told the story, he remembers driving on a street near our house. He was headed home after a night of bar hopping. He said that as he turned on to a nearby street, he heard a voice. It was as clear as if someone were sitting in the passenger seat of his jeep. He said that He was convinced that it was the audible voice of God. The voice said to him, "John, If you will follow me, I will save your life and deliver you from your addiction to alcohol." My dad said that he said, "Yes, I will follow you." He said that immediately he went from being an alcoholic to being completely sober. He found out later that my stepmother had been trying to track him down all night with the intent to kill him with a shotgun she was carrying in her car. My dad decided the very next day after his God encounter that as a family we all needed to learn about this God that had so powerfully impacted his life. So, the summer before I entered the 8th grade our family started to attend church.

I began to learn new things that helped me to change the way I faced life. I learned scriptures in the Bible that helped me with the nightmares and other things that were challenging my daily living.

I read in 2nd Timothy 1:7 that God has not given us a spirit of fear, but of power, love and a sound mind. Another scripture I read was Philippians 4:6-7. It says, "Be anxious for nothing, but in everything by prayer and supplication, with thanksgiving, let your requests be made known to God; and the peace of God, which surpasses all understanding, will guard your hearts and minds through Christ Jesus."

I learned that if I prayed, I could have peace, a peace so powerful that it would guard my heart and mind.

My mind! My mind! My mind! What an incredible thing to learn.

I began to pray before I would go to bed at night. I would pray for peace, and I would pray for good dreams. The prayer I prayed was something similar to this:

> "Dear God, I thank you for peace! I thank you for the peace that your Word says will guard my heart and mind. I pray that you would give me sweet sleep. I pray the blood of Jesus to protect me, and that as I lay down to sleep that your angels would minister to me in my sleep. I pray for pleasant dreams. And that I would wake up fully rested and refreshed."

The nightmares stopped! I believe that God will be just as merciful to you as He was to me. If you suffer from debilitating nightmares, pray this prayer each night before you lie down and go to sleep. I trust that you will receive the same freedom that I did.

I also began to see myself as God sees me instead of what others say that I am, or what others did to me. First Corinthians 13:12 NLT says, "Now we see things imperfectly, like puzzling reflections in a mirror, but then we will see everything with perfect clarity. All that I know now is partial and incomplete, but then I will know everything completely, just as God now knows me completely."

As I began to see myself through the mirror of God's word things began to change in my life. I was able to start the process of forgiveness. The biggest thing that helped me was realizing that God had extended forgiveness to me. And that in Matthew 6:14-15 it says that if we can't forgive, then we cannot expect forgiveness. Forgiveness is such a powerful thing! There is a saying that says, "Holding on to forgiveness in our lives is like drinking poison and expecting the other person to die." Forgiveness releases us more than it releases the other person. It's just as powerful when we have forgiveness extended to us. It's as if a weight is lifted off our shoulders. There is a new sense of freedom. So, at the age of twelve, sitting in a little church in the mountains of Lake Arrowhead, California, I made the decision to accept God's forgiveness and pray a simple prayer of salvation. Once I did that, it was the beginning of the most powerful freedom and transformation in my life.

This was what I prayed:

"Dear God, I want to be a part of your family. You said in Your Word that if I acknowledge that you raised Jesus from the dead and that I accept Him as my Lord and Savior, I would be saved. So God, I now say that I believe you raised Jesus from the dead and that He is alive and well. I accept Him now as my personal Lord and Savior. I accept my salvation from sin right now.

I ask you for your forgiveness, and I give you all my shame, guilt, and wrongdoing.

Thank you for forgiving me, accepting me, and embracing me.

I am now saved. Jesus is my Lord. Jesus is my Savior. Thank you, Father God, for forgiving me, saving me, and giving me eternal life with you. Amen!"

"Don't worry about anything,
instead pray about everything.
Tell God what you need and
Thank Him for all He has done.
Then you will experience God's
peace, which exceeds Anything we
can understand. His Peace will
guard your hearts and
Minds as you life in Christ Jesus."

Philippians 4:6-7 (NLT)

Chapter 7

ASHES, ASHES, WE ALL FALL DOWN

Marriage is an enigma. Does anyone really know what makes a good marriage? I don't think there is any one perfect way. We can look at the scriptures and see what the Bible says about husbands and wives. But in reality, every marriage is different. You can't give anyone a rulebook and say, this is what you have to do to have a perfect marriage. What works for one couple may not work for another.

At the time I met Eddie, I didn't think I wanted to date, we ended up spending a lot of time together, and we began to feel like marriage was in our future. We only dated for three months before he asked me to marry him and I said yes. Since I didn't live at home, I didn't want to ask for permission to get married, so we waited until I turned eighteen and we eloped.

We didn't tell any family. We only told two friends who stood as our witnesses. We found a 90-year-old minister in a nearby town who officiated weddings in his living room as his precious little wife played the organ. We laugh about it now, but we didn't have much money, so after the simple ceremony we went to McDonald's to celebrate by sharing a Happy Meal. It was such a spur of the moment thing that we hadn't even talked about where we would spend the night afterwards. So we went to Eddie's parent's house where he was living at the time. His mom was a very sweet conservative lady. She was happy for us, but she still asked to see the marriage license before she would allow me to stay and for us to sleep in the same room together. We didn't tell my dad until three days later. Needless to say, he was not happy because we robbed him of the opportunity to walk his only daughter down the aisle. We called my mom later in the week and she was happy for me.

We didn't have a honeymoon or a reception. Eddie and I were just so ready to move on the next phase of our lives that we didn't care about any of the fanfare. We just wanted to be married and get on with life. I don't know what we were thinking. We were just young and in love and thought we could figure it out along the way.

I think most of us start out seeking advice and wisdom from those who we admire. We read books; watched TV shows, read magazines. Anywhere and everywhere we are searching for answers to the perfect marriage. We even look to our friends and think, "Well, they look like they have a great marriage. Let's do what they're doing."

The problem is that each marriage is made up of different people, with different backgrounds, different histories, etc. It's important to discover what works for you! What works for your lifestyle, your work schedule, your family values, your level of fitness and activity.

Eddie and I thought we had it all figured out! We did everything right. We stood before God, our two witnesses, and the little minister who officiated our wedding and committed ourselves "for better, or for worse, 'til death do us part." Just thirteen months after getting married we welcomed our first son into the world. His little brother followed eighteen months after that. We had an adorable little family of four (at the time. Our third son would make his entrance into the world five and a half years later)! We were making things work for our little family, according to what we had been taught in church. We were involved in church, we read our Bible, we prayed. We were familiar with scriptures that talk about marriage. Little did we know that we were drifting apart.

One day, about three years into the marriage, I realized that I didn't feel like I loved my husband anymore. There wasn't a specific day. There wasn't a specific feeling. It just kind of snuck up on me.

I started feeling distant from him. I didn't miss him when he was at work. I didn't look forward to seeing him come home. I didn't desire to be intimate with him. I now understand how people feel when they said they "fell out of love" with someone. I was just enduring the marriage and going through the motions. But, I wasn't blaming him. I was the one that had a problem. I had made a commitment to God that divorce wasn't an option. Eddie and I had agreed before we even exchanged vows that divorce would not even a part of our vocabulary. So, I was stuck! What was I going to do? We had two small boys, and I had to figure something out.

I realize that in today's society if a person falls out of love with their spouse they figure that the best step to take is getting a divorce, but I think that is too easy of an out! First of all, most people I know while getting married made vows before friends and family and said words like, "for better or for worse, till death do us part." It causes me to think, Didn't you mean what you said? I wasn't willing to give up so easily. And anyway, it was my problem, not his! For all I knew, he was still happy and in love with me. It was just me. So what's a girl to do? I went to God. After all, it was God that I committed to.

From the beginning, I told my husband that it was important that each of us loved God more than we loved each other. It was important to me that we had our priorities in order, and if God were number one in our lives, then everything else would fall in line. God first! Then my husband. This began my journey of seeking God to help me fix what was broken. Namely me!

I remember so clearly taking some time while Eddie was at work, and the boys were taking a nap I got alone in my living room and went back to the basics of what I knew. I opened my Bible up to Ephesians 5:21-33. This talks about the husband's and wife's responsibilities in marriage. This has nothing to do with whether or not my husband was doing his part. This was the best place to start. I had to check myself to see if I was keeping up my end of the deal. Was I doing all I could do to nurture my feelings of love, respect, admiration, and affection toward my husband? (I didn't share my struggles with him at the time because it wasn't his issue, it was mine.) The next thing I did was to speak a prayer that I would pray daily, sometimes even hourly (or whenever the idea of not loving my husband would try to creep into my thoughts.)

This was the simple prayer that I would pray: "Dear God, I pray that you would help me to love my husband again. Please love him through me until I can learn to love him again on my own."

I don't remember the exact amount of time that I prayed this. It could've been weeks or months. All I know is that I began to love my husband again! It was a slow process, but as I worked on my wifely commandments found in Ephesians 5, and continued to pray my heartfelt prayer to God, things began to change. So what are some of those wifely commandments found in Ephesians 5? Simply put:

1. Submission: most women hate this word, but in reality, all it means is that you have the same goals, you are going the same direction as your husband. Not being resistant to the goals and vision for the marriage and family.

2. Be subject to your husband: basically, be on the same team.

3. Respect: men need respect like women need romance. Let him be your superhero!

Did my husband change? No! I changed. My attitude, my actions, and my heart all began to change slowly, and that's what made the difference.

To be honest, I don't even think Eddie knew there was ever any problem until I began to speak about it at different speaking engagements. It probably came as a surprise the first time he heard it. I didn't think, at the time, that it would be fair to put the responsibility on him to fix the situation because it wasn't his problem. So I never told him how I was feeling. But I know that when I began sharing it during some of my speaking engagements he was happy to hear that I kept God as the focus in the midst of challenges in my life.

Today we are enjoying thirty-three years of marriage. We now have three sons, two daughters-in-law, a beautiful granddaughter, and a grandson on the way. Is our life perfect? No. But, coming from a recovering perfectionist, I believe that perfection is an unrealistic expectation that many people strive for. And unfortunately, they are setting themselves up for disappointment and adding unnecessary pressure on themselves and their spouses.

Is there ever a happy ending? Well, let me just say that I'm saving that for another chapter later in the book.

"Dear God I pray that you would help me to love my husband again. Please love him through me until I can learn to love him again on my own."

Chapter 8

THE HIGHER THE HEEL, THE CLOSER TO GOD

A girl needs her shoes, right!? That's what I always believed. I've been known for wearing high heels since I was in high school, probably because I'm so short! Remember, at my best, I only hit 5'2".

There is a saying in Texas that says, "The higher the hair, the closer to God." But I like to say, "The higher the heel, the closer to God." But in all reality, I guess getting closer to God has been a search from the beginning of time. People are trying to figure out what they can do to get closer to God. You can see that even in the story of the tower of Babel when they were trying to build a tower that reached all the way to heaven.

I completely understand the desire to get closer to God and do anything you can to get there. But for me, I always felt like the closer I was to the ground, the closer I could get to God. Because of that, many times in prayer I get on my knees or even lie face down. Some people have a prayer chair. But I can take any piece of floor and make it my prayer spot. Prayer has always been important to me, even from a young age, along with worship, of course. There is this incredible desire that I've always had on the inside of me to draw closer to God. To do anything I can to see Him, feel Him, and experience Him, through prayer, through worship, and spending time alone reading His Word. I just want to be as close to Him as possible.

I realize that to some people prayer is a scary thing. They don't know how to pray, or what to say. What helped me is when I realized that God simply wants a relationship with us. He wants to have ongoing conversations with us. Just like we do with our dear friends and family. It's not about having the right words, or the correct formula, or even being in a specific position. It's about talking to Him as if He were sitting right next to you and speaking in your normal, everyday language that you use in your daily communication with those you care about. So I just started talking. Talking about what made me happy and made me sad. Sharing my good times and my bad times. Telling Him about my frustrations as well as my joys. And I began to mark out appointments in my calendar to talk to Him.

Just like in any relationship, it's important to make time. So, at first, I would mark times in my calendar to spend with God to pray and read the Bible. It helped me to make appointments until it became more of a naturally occurring thing. It has now become a regular thing to talk with God. I'm sure that there are times that people think I'm having a conversation with myself. Are there times when I spend more specific time in focused prayer? Yes, absolutely! And I have no specific time that I pray. Just whenever I feel a need to pray for something, I pray.

I never really had a close relationship with my dad. So, that may be part of it—just that desire of a little girl wanting to have her daddy around.

The dynamic of a father's influence is interesting! The level of security and peace in a child's life is directly affected by the presence of a father or lack thereof.

I'm grateful that I married a man that has done his best to be a good father. Especially since we have three sons! I was such a girly girl growing up that I had no idea how to raise boys. And since Eddie was a two-time world champion skateboarder, our boys were encouraged to be active.

I think that most people understand that there is no such thing as a perfect father as only God Almighty can fill that role. The girl who grows up having a comfortable, communicative, relationship with her Godly father generally has advantages over other girls regarding:

- Getting close to God early in life;

- Early exposure to the Scriptures and ability to imbibe Godly doctrines;

- Being self-confident and building self-esteem;

- A willingness to be innovative and accept challenging tasks; and

- Asserting her opinions and standing up for her beliefs;

You'll be glad to know that you, daughter, have a Father in heaven Who is the epitome of perfection. He does have a perfect plan for you. "For I know the thoughts that I think toward you, says the LORD, thoughts of peace and not of evil, to give you a future and a hope." Jeremiah 29:11 (NKJV).

Even at times when it may feel that he is nowhere around, He will never leave you stranded: "teaching them to observe all things that I have commanded you; and lo, I am with you always, even to the end of the age" Matthew 28:20 (NKJV).

DAWNA ELGUERA

"Give a girl

the right pair of shoes

and she can

conquer the world!"

Marilyn Monroe

Chapter 9

DEFYING THE LAW OF GRAVITY

It seems as though things around us are designed to bring us down, more than lift us up. In all reality, gravity is for our benefit. It keeps our feet planted on the ground instead of floating around in space. But it would be wonderful if we could be surrounded by more uplifting things than things that drag us down!

The truth of it all is that we must work at surrounding ourselves with positive, uplifting people and situations. But what happens when you can't get out of the circumstances that you are in? That seemed to be my reality for most of my childhood and teen years. It wasn't until my early teens that I realized that I could change my inward focus. Change my inward perspective. And when I do that, it doesn't necessarily affect my outward situation, but it does change how my outward circumstances affect me. There is a saying that goes, "Life is 10% circumstances and 90% how you react." In other words, you can't always change what is going on around you, but you can change how you respond to your circumstances.

I changed how I THOUGHT about my circumstances. I changed how I RESPONDED to my circumstances. I changed the negative thought process that tried to occupy my mind. I took back the power and control of what I could control…my attitude! I guess you could say I defied gravity. Nothing was going to pull me down anymore. The only way THAT would happen again was if I allowed it. I had to begin catching myself when negative thoughts began to overtake my thought process. When I would catch myself in negative thoughts, I would make a conscious decision to stop the negative thought process and focus on something positive. I would try to identify positive aspects of whatever circumstance I was dealing with at the time.

I realize that may sound unrealistic or that I don't understand how hard it can be not to be down, or depressed, or feel hopeless when dealing with an abusive situation. But I'm not trying to give you "pie in the sky" concepts that are unachievable. On the contrary, I want to encourage you, inspire you, and empower you to believe that you can be more than what has been said or done to you. You have a power on the inside of you to rise above adversity!

I don't know where you're at in your situation right now. You may be right in the middle of it, or it may be part of your past. You may still struggle with residual effects even if you are out of the situation now.

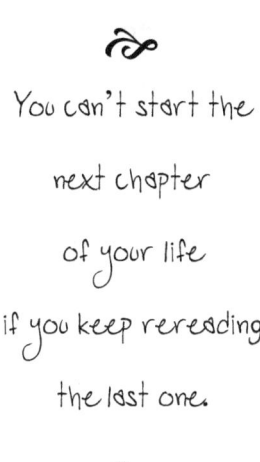

You can't start the

next chapter

of your life

if you keep rereading

the last one.

But if anything comes from me sharing my story with you, it would be that someone would find the power to break off every last thing that might be holding you back, holding you down, or whispering in your ear that you don't deserve any better than what you have right now.

I pray that as you read this, you are feeling me tapping you on the shoulder saying, "Tag, you're it! It's your time to shine!" I hope there is a stirring inside of you to take a step forward from where you've been. Step out of your comfort zone and believe that you are worth reaching for the stars!

I pray that as you read this, there is a stirring on the inside of you! A little bit of fear, and a little bit of courage. It's just enough for you to sit up a little taller and say, "I'm worth it! I can do this!" Let's reach for the stars!

I believe that there is a level of greatness on the inside of you that you haven't even tapped into yet. You may not have realized that it's there. But it is I guarantee you it's there.

What is it that you've always dreamed of? Is it a particular job, a place to visit, a place to live? What is it that excites you, motivates you? Why not go after it? You can do it! Refuse to let others hold you back and pull you down anymore.

It's your time to defy gravity and soar above the norm. Soar above the limitations that have been placed on you.

Chapter 10

THEY LIVED HAPPILY EVER AFTER

My story isn't finished and neither is yours. I believe that women are resilient! Our hearts can be stepped on and broken, yet we can bounce back with the ability to love again. I believe this is because women have a prophetic ability to see beyond what a person currently is and see what that person can become.

Women play a very special part in the story of humanity. What a beautiful thought it is that God recognized man's need for a suitable companion and that God's solution to this problem was the creation of a woman. Picture God's thought process with me for a moment: The first woman was created from a rib that God removed from the first man, Adam. This signified that the woman was created to protect the heart of man. The woman was designed to be by man's side, as a companion, not his enemy or his punching bag.

Women were created with the nature of God, caring, compassionate, and discerning. But also strong, tenacious, able to handle not only emotional and psychological pain but also the excruciating pain of childbirth. Women are an incredible creation!

Having devoted my life to speaking to people, empowering people, and listening to people, I can tell you that we women are soft, we are caring, we can accommodate, we can endure, if we want to, and we can also get loosed. Loosed in the sense that, when we have been pushed too far, and we can't take it anymore, we have the capacity to stand up and say, "Enough!"

There are women who have been in relationships but cannot find happiness. My heart breaks to hear or see women in such situations. Do you know the strength you possess as a woman? The story of women throughout history is one of strength and endurance, not weakness. That's the kind of power and strength you possess.

Mind you, your God-given strength can make and can destroy, but as a Christian woman, you must use that strength positively. For example, when I realized I didn't love my husband anymore, you will see how I applied that strength in my marriage in order to love my husband once again. It was true that I didn't feel like I loved him any longer, but he didn't realize that until much later. I didn't believe it would be fair to put the responsibility on him to fix it because it wasn't his problem. So I never told him how I was feeling. I know you will ask, "How?" Yes, some women would begin to act weird once the love is no longer there. By doing so, the marriage may collapse, but I took it to God and He saw me through.

Let me shock you a little bit. Do you know, as a woman, you are the pillar and bridge of your marriage? Oh yes, you are. Once you make that vow in the presence of family and friends, no going back. You have God on your side! He's the very One who could help you daily learn how to handle matters in your marital life.

Many times, men may behave contrary to what you may think is right, but how do you react? Your ability to handle issues in mature and unexpected ways makes him love you more.

To be sincere, I am saying this out of experience. Be a woman of valor, act like those women in the Bible; Esther, Hannah, and Sarah. If you are a woman who finds it difficult to enjoy your marriage, don't give up! Don't walk away! Take it to God in prayer. If you are a woman who finds it difficult to understand your man, take it to God in prayer.

I talked about having strength as a woman, yes, but do not be like Jezebel and Delilah, who were out to destroy men whom God elected for a purpose. Be like the daughters of Zion, those who were beautiful, wise, prayerful, discerning, prudent, patient, kind, and loyal.

You have the power to draw your man closer to God; the power to quench the fire of misunderstanding and strife in your home and live happily ever after.

My story of happily ever after is still being written, as is yours. I don't want you to give up during the hard times! I don't want you to ever think that what happened in your past defines or determines what your future will be.

Jeremiah 29:11 tells us, "For I know the thoughts that I think toward you, says the Lord, thoughts of peace and not of evil, to give you a future and a hope."

I believe that we all have an enemy. Satan himself is the enemy of all humanity. And his goal is to grab hold of us and ruin our lives in childhood so that he can continue to twist and destroy our futures. He uses people to do it.

But there is an incredible truth in that we have the power to rewrite our story. God has given us a future and a hope for better things. Someone may have exerted their power over us, but we have the ability to take our power back. Don't let anyone else write your story.

Take the power back; rewrite your story! Write yourself as the hero who destroys the monster. You have the power to change the narrative of your life. You win! You overcome the monster!

Today doesn't have to be as hard as yesterday was. And tomorrow doesn't have to be as challenging as today is. Your tomorrow can be different. Your future can be different.

You have a beautiful future ahead of you. But you must stand up, beautiful daughter of God. Believe that you deserve an incredible life. Ultimately you choose what your future will be. You can choose your happily ever after story.

♡ur growing family in 2017

Notes

1. "Abuse." *West's Encyclopedia of American Law, edition 2*. The Gale Group, Inc., 2008. http://legal-dictionary.thefreedictionary.com/abuse Accessed May 28 2017.

2. "Child Abuse." *West's Encyclopedia of American Law, edition 2*. The Gale Group, Inc., 2008. http://legal-dictionary.thefreedictionary.com/Child+Abuse Accessed May 28 2017.

3. "Child Abuse," *Learners Dictionary, Merriam-Webster*, (n.d.) http://www.learnersdictionary.com/definition/abuse Accessed May 28 2017.

About the Author

Dawna's amazing story of survival and strength is inspiring. She learned that her hardships do not define her. Instead, they have become the pages of her life story. It is a story that she shares with others as she travels the world to bring hope, healing and freedom to others.

Dawna has been married to Pastor Eddie Elguera, for the past 33 years. Raised in Lake Arrowhead, California, she has been in full-time ministry for almost 30 years. During that time her responsibilities included being youth pastor with her husband, women's ministry administrator, and School of Ministry instructor and Co-Senior Pastor with her husband for the past 12 years.

Over the past two decades, Dawna and her family have traveled throughout North America, Central and South America, Europe, Australia, and Asia through various missions and ministry opportunities.

In 2006, she and her husband were launched into the adventure of co-pastoring and leading The Rock Church in the Palm Springs area. She loves the full life God has entrusted to her and enjoys navigating the adventure of marriage, motherhood, being a grandmother, ministry and the momentum that Kingdom life presents. Her strong leadership gift and her commitment to excellence fuels her commitment to teaching the Word of God with a lively, inspiring and practical approach so that all who hear would be motivated to expand their capacity to reach their God-given potential in Christ.

For more information regarding having Dawna speak:

DawnaElguera.com

Or

The Rock Church

75400 Gerald Ford Dr. Ste. 110

Palm Desert CA 92211

www.ingramcontent.com/pod-product-compliance
Lightning Source LLC
Chambersburg PA
CBHW070622050426
42450CB00011B/3104